The God of Times and Seasons:

Knowing What to do With Times and Seasons and Acting on it to Derive Maximum Benefits

DR. SIMEON AGBOLABORI

ARPress

ARPress
45 Dan Road Suite 5
Canton MA 02021
Hotline: 1(888) 821-0229
Fax: 1(508) 545-7580

Ordering Information:
Quantity sales. Special discounts are available on quantity purchases by corporations, associations, and others. For details, contact the publisher at the address above.

Printed in the United States of America.

ISBN-13:   Softcover 979-8-89676-195-2
                eBook   979-8-89676-196-9

Library of Congress Control Number: 2025917303

TABLE OF CONTENTS

FOREWORD

This book reveals clear examples of many individuals' value propositions in and dispositions to life; their victories, successes and the paths they took to achieve divine intentions for their seasons.

The book clearly explains "time" as an intrinsic part of life that transits between two events to create valuable changes within its path. Time, as in, "Chronos" orders the activities of man on Earth. It is characterized by seconds, minutes, hours and days. Within time are events and without events, time is of no essence. Time can be momentary or transitional. As a result, it must be valued and experienced.

On the other hand, "seasons" refer to a collection of history in a period of time within several earth-changing positions that create patterns. Seasons are periodical and last for a moment in time; hence their arrival always looks like the new normal. Seasons also vary, just as the rainy, winter and summer seasons.

God stands with you in your life per moments, events and seasons. Be it a second, an hour, a period, a year or even a lifetime. God transitions with us through times and seasons. He lives in time and outside of time, in seasons and out of seasons.

This book also enumerates these transitions as changing paradigms because as seasons change, reasons change and as such, believers must be open to the changes that each season offers. You can't fit God within the box of repetitions or cycles. He begins the cycles, lives in the cycles and determines the end of the cycles.

In this book, you will find that life comes with opportunities and whenever opportunities present themselves, they always require a prepared vessel. Here, preparation means mental, physical, emotional, financial and spiritual preparation. And, as it is usually said, a miracle emerges when an opportunity meets a prepared vessel. So many are rich or poor, happy or sad today as a result of their responses to opportunities presented.

For some, it's because they do not understand the time or seasons of their lives nor do they obey divine leading. For this reason, they have remained poor, sad and miserable. On the other hand, some became rich, joyful and successful because they understood and obeyed the times and seasons they were in and took advantage of opportunities that came their way.

Very importantly, this book highlights the function and importance of our responses to the seasons of our life.

As you move into different seasons of life, this book calls you to:

1. Invest wisely; in knowledge, assets and people.

2. Seek to understand your seasons. Why are you in that season? Its duration? How can you leverage the season? Etc.

3. Prepare for the next season before it emerges.

4. Stay in your lane. Pray and build.

5. Be systematic, methodical and spontaneous. Rigidity limits progress.

God never told us the journey would be rosy and without challenges. Yet, with our challenges, we can produce a life of purpose and victory in Christ Jesus.

Oluseyi Oyedele,
Dominion Family International,
Houston, Texas, USA.

DEDICATION

To Professor David Olowokere Ph.D., and his darling wife, Engineer Omoshalewa Olowokere for their outstanding professional practices and unquestionable Christian faith. Your constant support and encouragement to my vision and ministry are deeply appreciated.

To the evergreen memories of Apostle Moses Olowokere Agbolabori and Deaconess Julianah Adunni Wuraola Agbolabori who devoted their bodies, souls and spirits to serving the Lord and were founders and primates of the Spiritual Jesus Christ Apostolic Church, Nigeria. They served as examples of dedication to the Lord and their lives inspired me always to do more for the Lord.

Acknowledgments

The following people have made a significant impact and contribution to my life and ministry:

Pastor Sylvester and Pastor (Mrs.) Lola Oyeye of Mountain of Prayer and Praise International Ministries

Liberty Center Chapel in Houston Texas.

Pastors Remi and Angela Odueke of Royal House of Faith, Houston Texas.

Bishop Charles and Rev. (Mrs.) Olufunke Awowoyin of Christ Embassy International Ministries, Columbus, Ohio.

Evangelist (Dr.) Dan and Dr. (Mrs.) Patience Daniels of the Wealthy Place, Festac Town, Lagos, Nigeria.

Pastors John and Bridget Israel of Zion Covenant Ministries Houston, Texas.

Apostle Matthew and Pastor Covenant Oluwajoba of Christ United Ministries International, Houston, Texas.

Pastor Michael Osas and Pastor (Mrs.) Christy Okpamen of Abounding Love Christian Center, Stafford, Texas.

Pastor (Dr.) David B. Osho and Pastor (Mrs.) Esther Osho of International Way of Life Ministries, Houston, Texas

Thank you all for always making me feel loved and special. It is my prayer that God will make all good abound towards you and that you will have sufficiency in the name of Jesus Christ.

INTRODUCTION

"To everything there is a season, and a time to every purpose under the heaven" (Ecclesiastes 3:1).

When it comes to God, timing is everything. In life, there are times and seasons. Times and seasons are what make life beautiful and colorful. If you critically study the book of Ecclesiastes chapter 12, you will come to the frightening realization that nothing will last forever. In life, there are both natural and spiritual times and seasons.

In the natural, seasons come and go and we often appreciate those seasons based on how we feel about them. For example, those who love the winter season appreciate winter and despise summer and vice-versa.

Make no mistake about this. Neither summer nor winter cares about who likes them or who doesn't, but they come and go as they have been commanded by the Lord. Genesis 8:22 says, *"While the earth remaineth, seed-time and harvest, and cold and heat, and summer and winter, and day and night shall not cease"*

This understanding should make you to be seriously concerned about maximizing your seasons. You must realize that you are in this life for a reason, purpose and season. Make your life count. Make your mark in your world. You are timed. Have you ever experienced the tragedy, the hurt or the emptiness of losing someone you love? It does not matter the age they were, or how long they were here, you still felt the void in your life when their death occurred.

These people have fulfilled their purpose and they are gone. Just like the natural seasons, death does not give us a choice when God tells it to do its job. When Heaven calls your number, there is nothing like a missed call. Therefore, it is very important to maximize your moments with people and celebrate them while you have them, so that you don't have to live with both sorrow and regret when they are gone.

Most times we take our health for granted, until we hear the doctor's report that something does not sound well or look good. Sometimes we take our spouse for granted, until we stand by their casket, full of regret for not spending enough time or not learning enough from them before they went on to be with the Lord.

One of the ways you can maximize your seasons is to realize that times and seasons in the natural never return the same. Also, once a season, opportunity or year passes by, you can never get it again.

For times and seasons to work in your favor, it is vital that you seize the moments and redeem the time that God has given to you. There is nothing worse or wasteful than trying to work, plant and labor in the wrong season and time. One of the laws of harvest in agriculture is that you must plant the right crops in the right season.

There are certain seasons for you to plant certain things. If you plant out of season, you will not get the maximum harvest. Stop wasting your seed.   Be sensitive to discern the right season and the right soil to plant your seed. Our Father works according to times and seasons. Even when God gives you a prophetic word, it is important you realize that it is for a time and a season.

Little wonder Prophet Habakkuk said, *"I will stand upon my watch, and set me upon the tower, and will watch to see what he will say unto me, and what I shall answer when I am reproved."*

"And the LORD answered me, and said, Write the vision, and make it plain upon tables, that he may run that readeth it."

"For the vision is yet for an appointed time, but at the end it shall speak, and not lie: though it tarry, wait for it; because it will surely come, it will not tarry."

(Habakkuk 2:1-3)

This implies that we have to be patient but sensitive not to miss our season or get comfortable with our current positions and situations.

Here, then, are the fundamental truths you should know about times and seasons:

- God ordained times and seasons; hence, He is the God of times and seasons.

- Understanding times and seasons will make you checkmate the errors of your life.

- Time gives you space to correct your errors as a single mistake can take you many years and even a lifetime to correct.

- Time prepares you for the challenges ahead.

- Nothing will take you unawares if you understand times and seasons.

- Understanding times and seasons will position you for opportunities and align you with His divine agenda.

- Times and seasons afford you a chance in the factory where your destiny is produced.

- Times and seasons are bedrocks for your destiny to be fulfilled.

"There is an evil which I have seen under the sun, as an error which proceedeth from the ruler" (Ecclesiastes 10:5).

CHAPTER ONE

THE GOD WHO ALTERS TIMES AND SEASONS

Have you ever asked yourself these questions?

- *What season am I in?*
- *What is God's purpose for me in this season?*

Or do you just live as the days come, not seeking to know why things are happening at the time they are happening?

There is a time and season for everything. And having this understanding is crucial for your life. Daniel understood this life principle, and the Bible provides us with some proofs of this.

Daniel 2:20-22, for example, tells us: *"Daniel answered and said, Blessed be the name of God for ever and ever: for wisdom and might are his:. And he changeth the times and the seasons: he removeth kings, and setteth up kings: he giveth wisdom unto the wise, and knowledge to them that know understanding: He revealeth the deep and secret things: he knoweth what is in the darkness, and the light dwelleth with him.*

Our Heavenly Father is the God of times and seasons. He determines the times and seasons of your life. As a child of God, nothing happens to you by chance. There is nothing that happens to you that takes God by surprise. Naturally speaking, the moon and the sun were created to illuminate the Earth and to separate the day from night. They were to serve as signs to mark seasons, such as days and years.

Time is a temporary interruption in eternity. It is a commodity that can neither be bought nor sold. You can only maximize and utilize it. If you don't use it, you will lose it. You choose!

GOD'S INSTRUMENTS

Times and seasons are God's ordained instruments of measurement, assessment, planning and perfection. God uses time as an effective tool to plan and execute His plans. With time, everything that has a beginning must have an end. If God did not order everything to be in times and seasons, there will be no end to evil, wickedness, poverty, corruption, etc. And if the earth was designed to be like heaven - a timeless realm where change is impossible, unpleasant circumstances would never cease. Nothing would change.

But with time, change is possible. Anything you do not want can be eliminated.

With time, nothing is permanent - "no condition is permanent."

With time, failure can become success.

With time, a child can become an adult.

With time, the sick can experience wholeness.

With time, the imprisoned and oppressed can become delivered to reign in life.

With time, what you do not see in your today can be seen in your tomorrow.

What is the essence of these examples? **You can take advantage of times and seasons to change your circumstances, and in turn, put in place what you long to see that is not in existence.** Redeem the time, don't waste it! Make the most of every opportunity and do not let your God-given opportunities slip from your hands.

"Redeeming the time because the days are evil" (Ephesians 5:16).

MAXIMIZING CHANGE

As the saying goes, change is constant. It is inevitable. Times and seasons are the most powerful realities on earth. Whether you want it or not, you will experience change. In the last two years, we have witnessed massive global changes that hit the world. The Coronavirus disease that ravaged the whole world, affecting every sector, is an example.

"While we look not at the things which are seen, but at the things which are not seen: for the things which are seen are temporal; but the things which are not seen are eternal" (2 Corinthians 4:18).

The scriptures made a distinction between the "temporal" and the "eternal". Paul said that the things we can see are "temporal", that is, they are subject to change. And the things that we cannot see are "eternal", that is, they are constant - never changing.

Success in life is a product of how we leverage times and seasons. *"To everything, there is a season, and a time to every purpose under the heaven" (Ecclesiastes 3:1).* Therefore, at every point in your life, you have to be conscious of the season you are in, as your consciousness will help you maximize the purpose of your season. It is pathetic that most people often go through life without recognizing the seasons they are in. The absence of this recognition makes it difficult for them to prepare and maximize all that God has created for them in that season.

For every season, we must understand God's purpose for us within the timeline of that season. Also, we must draw from the lessons of that season as we wait to move into and engage the next season. Seasons are not static but dynamic; they keep changing. Therefore, it is crucial to understand and embrace them in our life journeys.

One of the greatest joys we have in this season is that we are in the Kairos of the Comforter - the Holy Spirit. As such, to experience divine encounters, we must maximize this season of the tremendous move of God by recognizing the finished work of Jesus Christ and the possibility of a deep relationship with the Holy Spirit. It is, therefore, crucial to align ourselves with God's purposes for us as we engage in the seasons of life.

10 THINGS YOU MUST KNOW ABOUT SEASONS

1. Every season needs a seed.
2. Every season comes with a change in atmosphere.
3. Seasons have a purpose.
4. Seasons have timings.

5. In every season, God is constant.
6. Each season has its unique purpose.
7. Everything in life is subject to seasons.
8. Seasons are cyclic/dynamic.
9. Each season is a gateway to the next season.
10. Every season comes with a prophetic urgency in the spirit.

God does not live or exist in time. God dwells in eternity. "Time" clearly does not relate to God and man in the same way. In describing this, the Psalmist declares in Psalm 90:4: *"For a thousand years in thy sight are but as yesterday when it is past, and as a watch in the night."*

Eternity is endless, but time is measured by a "beginning" and an "ending." In Genesis 1, the Bible commences with these words: *"In the beginning, God created the heaven and the earth."*

GOD IS IN CONTROL

The good news is that God is in control, no matter the changes. He is the same God with the same story! God still rules and reigns in the affairs of men.

We can see in the book of Daniel that God is in control, even of mighty human empires. Daniel said, *"He changes times and seasons, deposes kings and sets up kings."* (Daniel 2:21).

Daniel was God's man, strategically placed in Babylon. God revealed His plan for the nations to him. In chapter one, Daniel distinguished himself as a man of character. It takes character to secure a special place in God's heart.

Daniel was committed to a virtuous and righteous character and had set an uncompromising standard for his own life. Daniel had a supernatural ability and was vested with the knowledge, skill and wisdom that a leader needs to get to the top.

Truly, the God of Daniel is the God of sovereign power! He is the God who rules nations; He has the power to remove a king, and replace him with another. He has the power to crush the pride of earthly rulers. He is the God that reveals secrets. All the secrets of the universe are known to God. Everything in the past, present and future is known to God. He can tell the destinies of nations.

There is so much to learn about leadership in these times of global crisis. It is in these times we develop into the complete leader that God has destined each of us to become. Daniel was faced with such challenging situations. His leadership ability is a model for us to learn from.

At certain times, God used dreams to communicate with people. One of such people was King Nebuchadnezzar of Babylon. King Nebuchadnezzar reigned from 605 to 562

B.C. He greatly expanded the Babylonian Empire, conquered Jerusalem and took the Jews captive in the process. Daniel was one of those captives from Jerusalem and was granted access to education in the king's palace.

One night, Nebuchadnezzar had a troubling dream, in which God provided an overview of world events in the millennia yet to come. Though disturbed by the dream, there was another problem - he could not remember the dream. So, he called all his advisors together for a meeting. He ordered them to tell him both the dream and its meaning, threatening to kill them if they couldn't.

When these men answered that no one could tell the king his dream, Nebuchadnezzar commanded that all the wise men in Babylon be killed. Daniel was among those to be slain. This was standard procedure in a culture that placed high importance on dreams and their meanings. However, he had added an unprecedented requirement: "Tell me my dream and interpret it as well."

When Daniel learned about the danger, he told the king's captain he would interpret the dream if the king would give him time. He asked his friends, Shadrach, Meshach, and Abednego, to pray with him. Then, Daniel waited for God to reveal the dream and save the lives of the advisors. God answered his prayer and gave him a replay of the dream and its interpretation. He went to the king with the interpretation and averted disaster.

The dream featured a huge and glorious statue of a man. Its head was "made of pure gold, its chest and arms of silver, its belly and thighs of bronze, its legs of iron, its feet partly of iron and partly of baked clay." Then a rock "not cut by human hands" hit the foot of the statue, and the whole image "became like chaff on a threshing floor," while the rock "became a huge mountain and filled the whole earth."

Daniel's divine interpretation explained that the statue represents a series of kingdoms, each less glorious than the one before, as indicated by the decreasing value of the metals. The first four kingdoms have been identified as the Babylonian, Persian, Greek and Roman Empires. This identification has come from the workings of history, matching further prophecies. Daniel already said that Babylon, specifically Nebuchadnezzar, was the head of gold. Babylon fell to the kingdom of the Medes and Persians. Greece became the successor to the Medo-Persian Empire. The "iron" empire could only be Rome. As we know, four of these kingdoms have come and gone.

Daniel went on to say that the last empire, which was made of iron and clay, would be a divided kingdom and would be partly strong and partly broken. *"They shall not cleave to one another"* (Daniel 2:43b). In the days of this empire, God will destroy it and set up an everlasting Kingdom. Now we know that God has not destroyed it because God has not set up His everlasting Kingdom "yet". So, this partly iron and partly clay, 10-unit (10 toes) empire, is in the future (the Antichrist's empire).

King Nebuchadnezzar was shocked that Daniel was able to both tell him his dream and interpret it. He fell to the ground and worshipped Daniel. He said, "I now know that Daniel's God is the only TRUE God." The king was pleased, and as a reward, he made Daniel and his friends, rulers in Babylon.

When God granted Daniel the wisdom to interpret the king's dream, it launched Daniel's long career as a political leader, trusted advisor, and well-known prophet. He was clothed with divine knowledge, wisdom, intelligence, and supernatural understanding.

Daniel was ten times better than the so-called wise men in the Babylonian kingdom. He never compromised his godly standards, despite reigning amid Babylonians. He was blameless in all his ways. Daniel's positive character traits extinguished the diabolic schemes of his fervent opponents. He never allowed his detractors to dilute his focus.

UNDERSTANDING THE TIMES

There is no doubt the entire world is in a state of confusion. Will the world ever be like it was? There is no political answer to the challenges plaguing the human race. The reality is that it takes a real-life crisis to test our leadership capacity. Leading in these times of crisis demands that we focus on the root, not the fruit. What then is the root?

THE GOD-FACTOR

Daniel went to the king and asked for time to seek out God's help. It is hard to focus on the root of the problem when the fruit falls all around you and hits you on the head. However, the ultimate solution lies in the root. God was in control of this crisis and it was from Him the solution came.

"And of the children of Issachar, which were men that had understanding of the times, to know what Israel ought to do; the heads of them were two hundred; and all their brethren were at their commandment" (1 Chronicles 12:32).

The Bible says *"…the children of Issachar… had understanding of the times, to know what Israel ought to do."* In Israel, this was a crucial time. It was the period when the 11 tribes of Israel were without a leader, and therefore, lacked guidance and a model to follow. This tribe was distinguished in Israel because they understood the times. It is a tragedy to live in ignorance of the time you are living in.

When you have this understanding, you will know how to live and fit into God's agenda for the now. God is a planner, and no planning is done without a time frame. God schedules everything. Therefore, it is important that you and I understand the times that we are in at each point in our lives. This calls for diligence in searching out the program and timings of God, especially for our individual lives.

It is a time for special understanding. It is a time for real discernment. What did the men of Issachar understand? They understood the times when things normally took place. Also, they knew when it was time for a specific event to happen. They were able to interpret God's written Word by recognizing the significance of past events and applying the lessons to the present and the future.

It was a crucial time because it was destined that David should be king over all of Israel. David needed such men during this time in Israel's history. The men of Issachar would understand what God was about to do and would be a wonderful help in establishing the new kingdom. They would see to it that David did not fail to accomplish the task of integrating the entire kingdom under his reign.

As believers in Christ, we must be connected to God to discern the times and seasons that we live in. People who are deeply rooted in God are committed, courageous, fruitful, and exemplary. Trees require roots and branches. A tree must abide in its roots before it can bear fruits. Trees draw strength, values, and virtues from their roots. God is our taproot. Genesis 1:1 says, *"In the beginning God created the heavens and the earth."* His Word is our secondary root (John 1:5; Rev. 5:5).

It is our connectedness to the Root that determines our greatness in all facets of life. A tree that is not connected to its roots will eventually die.

BACK TO THE ROOT

It is common knowledge that the function of a product is dictated by its manufacturer, especially through the manual. God created the universe, including everything in and under the heavens. Therefore, it is impossible to rightly govern a nation without divine guidance and protection. That is, without full dependence on God and His Word.

George Washington, the first president of the USA, said, "It is impossible to rightly govern the world without God and the Bible." We certainly cannot be smarter or wiser than our Creator. Whatever God does is forever, but the self-induced successes of human beings are shaky.

Look at the history of the most powerful nations like Egypt, the Babylonian Empire, the Persian Empire, Greece and the Roman Empire. Where are their powers today? They have all vanished from the face of the Earth. Though it is our time, we must humbly return to our roots, if we really want to attain anything of lasting value. God is ready to listen to us when we call upon Him in these chaotic moments.

2 Chronicles 7:14 says, *"If my people, who are called by my name, will humble themselves and pray and seek my face and turn from their wicked ways, then I will hear from heaven, and I will forgive their sin and will heal their land."*

WHAT CAN YOU SEE?

Vision can alter your destiny. You must see greatness in any challenge and opportunities in any trial. To realize your full destiny, you must engage the power of vision. Where there is no vision, the people perish.

Helen Keller, probably the most-recognized blind person who ever lived, was asked, "What could be worse than being born blind?" She said, "The only thing worse than being blind is having sight but no vision."

"Where there is no vision, the people perish: but he that keepeth the law, happy is he" (Proverbs 29:18).

This means that when people lack divine revelations of God and the future, they throw off self-control, personal discipline, and restraint. Vision is everything. **"Vision is the source of personal, corporate and national discipline."** King Solomon's statement captures the significant role vision plays in all aspects of our lives. "Nothing noble or noteworthy on earth was ever done without a vision. No invention, development, or great feat was ever accomplished without the inspiring power of this mysterious source called vision."

Vision makes the unseen visible and the unknown possible. It makes suffering and disappointment bearable as vision provides insight into the beautiful future beyond our present challenges. The challenges plaguing the advancement of nations of the world call for new visions.

When the right leaders and the right timing come together, incredible things will happen. The right action at the right time will produce success. No man or leader can escape the law of timing.

CHAPTER TWO

THE SEASON OF ISOLATION AND PREPARATION

Before a man can be used by God, he has to go through a season of isolation and preparation. In God's curriculum, preparation precedes manifestation. The season of preparation develops you for leadership and responsibility. In these times of chaos and moral failure, God plans to raise a firebrand generation. A generation without blemish or compromise.

More than ever, the world needs servants and kingdom leaders; true leaders whose passion is to serve and not to be served. God is raising leaders who can change the mindset and mentality of followers. Leaders who can propel action where there was hesitation; courage where there was cowardice; optimism where there was cynicism, and strength where there was weakness.

For everyone called by God, there is a season of preparation before manifestation. This pattern is seen throughout the Scriptures. The season of preparation is crucial. This is the time between the divine call and the fulfillment of the call; between a prophetic word and its fulfillment; between sowing a seed and reaping the harvest; between humbling yourself and being exalted.

FIVE KEY STAGES IN THE SEASON OF PREPARATION

1. The Pruning Phase

Pruning is a painful process of purification and preparation for greater productivity. It is not an enjoyable process. However, if we submit to God's process of pruning, we will emerge ready to produce much fruit. Jesus said this in John 15:1-2: *"I am the true vine, and My Father is the vinedresser. Every branch in Me that does not bear fruit He takes away; and every branch that bears fruit He prunes, that it may bear more fruit."* (NKJV). It is important to understand that the process of pruning is not to punish but prepare us for the fulfillment of God's purpose. The season of pruning creates the capacity for greater fruitfulness.

2. The Testing Phase

In the season of preparation, you will be tested. Your character will be tested. Your motives will be tested and hidden wicked motives will be brought to the surface. These tests will reveal our faithfulness in little things, as faithfulness is the cornerstone of character. Paul admonished that those who take on leadership positions must not be *"a novice, lest being puffed up with pride he falls into the same condemnation as the devil"* (1 Timothy 3:6). Then he said that those who aspire to be deacons must *"first be tested"* (1 Timothy 3:10). As God takes us through the refining process, His purpose is to bring us to the place where we can handle promotion. If we are promoted prematurely, pride may set in and cause us to fall.

3. The Waiting Phase (Hidd*-en from the Spotlight)

The preparation process includes a waiting phase. John the Baptist waited in the wilderness *"until the day of his manifestation to Israel."* Joseph waited in prison, hidden away from society. Abraham waited a whole 13 years for the fulfillment of God's promise.

Though we are not in a literal wilderness, it is as if God hides us. We have true gifts, but they are undiscovered by many. We have a true calling, but we are not received by the church. We have a sense of vision, but we are waiting for it to come to fruition.

4. Limited Influence Phase

During the season of preparation, you may have influence, but it is limited. David was called to be king - the most influential person in Israel. The prophet Samuel anointed him and declared that he was God's choice as the next ruler of Israel. After this, he was launched into a difficult season of preparation.

King Saul became obsessed with trying to kill David, and he found himself often on the run and in hiding. During this time, a group of 400 men pledged themselves to him and he became their leader. His influence was real, but it was limited to a much smaller number than he would lead if he was an active king.

5. Restricted Manifestation of Gifts Phase

In the season of preparation, your gifts begin to emerge. But they are limited by your circumstances, environment, and sometimes, those above you in leadership. During this time, it is normal to be in a situation that is not ideal for your gifts to function.

Joseph's gifts were real while he was in Potiphar's house as a slave and while he was in the prison. But they were restricted by their environment. One of the reasons for this dynamic is that in the season of preparation, God is often doing more *in* you than *through* you. We cannot control the seasons. We cannot end the season of preparation by our own will or desire. But we can cooperate with God in each season and trust Him to faithfully bring us to the next!

You need to go through this season of preparation to be a true leader. A leader can create a spirit of hope where there was despair. True leaders do the right things at the right time. Leadership determines the mentality, destiny, attitude, and commitment of the followers. Nothing changes without effective, sensitive and righteous leadership. Leadership is the cause of all our problems and also the solution to all our problems. You can only lead people to the degree of the future you have envisioned yourself.

Leadership means taking people from where they are to where they ought to be. The result of true leadership is discomfort and change. "The most important source of leadership is vision." Leadership never ends; only leaders end. Therefore, leaders should focus on developing future leaders. They should have deliberate succession plans; they must not just focus on immediate change but focus on those who will bring about change in the future.

The reason for followership is leadership. You follow a leader so that you can learn the intricacies of good leadership to become a leader. Leadership is the capacity to influence followers through spiritual insight motivated by divine passion, generated by a Godly vision, produced by a delightful conviction and ignited by a celestial purpose.

True leaders are upright people. They focus on how to overcome the real challenges of the society they lead. Such leaders selflessly and passionately design and implement strategic blueprints to meet the real needs of the people they serve. Joseph in the Bible is one of the greatest leaders of the Old Testament, second perhaps, to Moses. What made him stand out from others was his absolute integrity and trust in God, regardless of what happened to him. He is a shining example of what can happen when a person obeys God completely.

THE SEPARATION AND PREPARATION OF JOSEPH

Genesis 37:26-28: *"And Judah said unto his brethren, What profit is it if we slay our brother, and conceal his blood? Come, and let us sell him to the Ishmeelites, and let not our hand be upon him; for he is our brother and our flesh. And his brethren were content. Then there passed by Midianites merchantmen, and they drew and lifted up Joseph out of the pit, and sold Joseph to the Ishmeelites for twenty pieces of silver: and they brought Joseph into Egypt."*

One day, Joseph had a vision and told his brothers. The brothers who disliked Joseph because of their father's partial show of love for him disliked him even more. A few days later, Joseph's father asked him to check on his brothers. They were in the fields, quite a distance away. So Joseph went to find them.

When the brothers saw Joseph from a distance, they made a plan to kill him. So when Joseph came to them, they took off his beautiful robe and threw him into an empty well. A while later, a group of merchants on their way to sell some things in Egypt came by.

Then, one of the brothers spoke up, *"Why don't we sell him to these people? This way, we will never have to see him again and at the same time, we won't have to kill him."* This suggestion suited the other brothers, so they sold him to the merchants heading to Egypt. However, because they wanted to tell their father that Joseph was dead, they dipped Joseph's beautiful robe in animal blood and took it back to their father. When Jacob saw it, he cried, *"Some animal has killed my son."* He cried bitterly for many days but nobody could comfort him.

Meanwhile, Joseph had started as a slave in Egypt. However, the Lord was with Joseph and He helped him do everything right. After being taken to Egypt, Joseph was sold again to Potiphar, an official in Pharaoh's household. Through hard work and humility, Joseph rose to the position of overseer of Potiphar's entire estate. But Potiphar's wife lusted after Joseph. When Joseph rejected her sinful advance, she lied and accused Joseph of rape. Potiphar had Joseph thrown into prison.

Joseph must have wondered why he was being punished for doing the right thing. Even so, he worked hard again and was put in charge of all the prisoners. Because the Lord was with Joseph in jail, he never worried but trusted the Lord to help him act right. After Joseph had been in jail for some time, both the palace cupbearer and Pharaoh's baker were sent to prison as punishment for some undisclosed offences. One night, each of them had a dream and told Joseph their dreams.

Now, God had given Joseph the gift of interpreting dreams. He told the cupbearer that his dream meant he would be freed and returned to his former position. Joseph told the baker his dream meant he would be hanged. Both interpretations proved true. When the cupbearer was freed, he forgot about what Joseph did.

So, Joseph stayed in jail for two more years. One day, Pharaoh had a dream, and nobody could explain it to him. The cupbearer then remembered Joseph, and he was brought to Pharaoh. Of course, Joseph interpreted the dream and his God-given wisdom was so great that Pharaoh put him in charge of the whole of Egypt.

After Pharaoh had told him about his dream, Joseph explained:

"God is warning you. There will be a period of seven years when nothing will grow and there won't be any food for anyone."

"What can I do?" Pharaoh asked.

"God has shown you what to do. There will be seven good years in which everything would be in abundance and sufficient before the bad seven years. The seven good years would be so good that there will be extra food for everyone. So, you should save a little bit of each year's harvest, that way you will have enough to get you through the bad years." Joseph said.

Pharaoh believed all that Joseph told him and put him in charge of all the lands of Egypt.

People came from all countries to buy grain from Joseph because the entire world needed food. Some of these people who came to buy food were Joseph's brothers! When his brothers came, Joseph recognized them, but they did not know who he was. It had been over 10 years since they last saw him. The brothers all bowed to him because he had become important and powerful; just as he dreamed in the beginning that they would.

After a few meetings with his brothers, Joseph could not keep it in any longer and Joseph said to his brothers, *"I am Joseph! Is my father alive?"* But his brothers couldn't answer him because they were afraid. Then Joseph said, *"Come here. I am your brother, the one you sold! Do not worry, and do not be angry at yourselves for selling me, because God has put me here to save people from starving."* So his father, brothers, and their families came to live in Egypt with Joseph, and they had all the food they needed.

Joseph, as a wise prime minister, saved Egypt and the entire world from a potential nasty effect of a seven-year severe famine. His economic policies stood the test of time. Joseph remains the world's greatest economic adviser, wise planner, and selfless leader. He was entrusted with the wealth of Egypt - the then most powerful nation in the world; yet he was never accused of misappropriation or corruption. Therefore, he became an example of leadership with integrity and character. He demonstrated personal integrity and transparency.

Besides, Joseph never abused his authority. Although it was within his powers to retaliate against the wickedness of his elder brothers, he showed mercy and sought their welfare. Joseph preferred reconciliation to revenge. He walked in the counsel of the Lord.

11 OUTSTANDING QUALITIES THAT DEVELOPED IN THE LIVES OF DANIEL AND JOSEPH DURING THEIR SEASONS OF PREPARATION

God used the season of preparation to develop and prepare both Joseph and Daniel for leadership and responsibility. They developed the following outstanding qualities in their seasons of isolation and preparation:

1. They were blameless leaders in all ramifications.

2. They had personal knowledge of God.

3. They had spiritual sensitivity.

4. They acknowledged God's presence in all situations.

5. They completely relied on God and looked unto Him at every moment.

6. They sought God's guidance before taking any step or decision.

7. They obeyed the laws of God to the letter.

8. They applied God's word to their own lives and in everything they did.

9. They had forgiving and pure hearts.

10. They chose to serve their generations rather than lord over the people or seek their personal welfare.

11. They subjected their authority to God's authority.

It is worth noting that the qualities these exemplary leaders demonstrated can only be found in God. Education and much learning can never produce them. Technology is never a substitute for these indispensable qualities. No form of human training and teachings can cure sin, corruption, greed, dishonesty, wickedness, etc.

Human systems do not have the right force to promote law and order. Besides, no human-based organization can secure and maintain true world unity and peace. Charismatic leadership is never a substitute for character-based leadership.

True leadership is in towels, not in titles. Leadership is about serving the best interest of others. Jesus Christ exemplified this kind of leadership when He washed His disciples' feet. To sacrifice His models and principles of leadership for human ideologies will amount to multiplying our sorrows. His leadership principles and acts are undeniably the best. They are divine, reliable, workable and lasting. Joseph and Daniel used these principles and they succeeded.

Throughout the pages of the Bible, God and His inspired scribes have penned the stories of men and women chosen to lead His people. Some, like Daniel and Joseph, demonstrated good leadership, while others stumbled. When we look closely at their stories, we can identify the characteristics needed for leadership.

These men and women who led correctly had faith and trust in God, humility, patience, courage, wisdom, kindness toward mankind, and strength.

They were not leaders for the title but were leaders called to take on the responsibility of activating change for the common good. In essence, national and religious leaders must be men and women whose characters are trustworthy and esteemed highly by their community. Such men and women are known for their wholesome life and untarnished integrity. They are men and women of good character and reputation.

CHAPTER THREE

ENGAGING YOUR SEASONS AND ACTIVATING THE HARVEST

THE ISSACHAR GENERATION

"And of the children of Issachar, which were men that had understanding of the times, to know what Israel ought to do; the heads of them were two hundred; and all their brethren were at their commandment" (1 Chronicles 12:32).

"For thus saith the LORD of hosts, the God of Israel; The daughter of Babylon is like a threshing floor, it is time to thresh her: yet a little while, and the time of her harvest shall come" (Jeremiah 51:33).

You have the right to expect a harvest when you have sown seeds.

THE SEASON OF PLANTING AND HARVEST

Every season has a purpose. Understanding the purpose of the seasons of your life is critical. No matter the season God places you in, sowing is very vital. Before you can harvest, there has to be a time you planted. There is always a time for the growth of the seed being planted. This is where patience is required. It is a season of waiting in anticipation. However, growth leads to elevation.

The planting season is a season of giving without receiving. It is a time of hard work, a time to crucify self, a time of sacrifice and a time to diligently serve. It is also a time of working in obscurity. To some, this is the wilderness experience. The harvest season is a time of manifestation, breakthroughs, and projection! Your work will announce you even when you do not want to show off.

Spiritually speaking, seasons can be activated. There are principles that God has ordained to activate seasons in our lives. God created the world and ordered its operations, including the times and seasons of men. So, there is a time to plant and a time to harvest. In other words, there is a season for everything.

Ecclesiastes 3:1, 4-8 says:

"To every thing there is a season, and a time to every purpose under the heaven:

"A time to weep, and a time to laugh; a time to mourn, and a time to dance; A time to cast away stones, and a time to gather stones together; a time to embrace, and a time to refrain from embracing;

A time to get, and a time to lose; a time to keep, and a time to cast away; A time to rend, and a time to sew; a time to keep silence, and a time to speak;

A time to love, and a time to hate; a time of war, and a time of peace."

It is a fatal error to pray for a harvest when you've not planted any seed or labored in any way. No seed, no harvest. The sowing of seeds always precedes a harvest.

RECOGNIZING YOUR SEASONS

This is vital. The ability to recognize your seasons is one of the factors that will qualify you for manifestation. The recognition of your season is a call to action. When God in His mercies decides to visit you at your set time, you must not be careless to take the time of visitation for granted or despise such a time. It is your responsibility to take appropriate actions at such times.

"While the earth remaineth, seedtime and harvest, and cold and heat, and summer and winter, and day and night shall not cease" (Genesis 8:22).

"Do not be deceived, God is not mocked; for whatever a man sows, that he will also reap" (Galatians 6:7).

God has set in place the season of seedtime and harvest. The size of your seed determines the capacity of your harvest. The first and core principle of seedtime and harvest is that you will get what you planted or sowed. The Bible says, "you reap what you sow." This is true both from a negative and positive perspective. If you plant disorder and trouble, you will reap disorder and trouble. If you plant peace and harmony, you will experience peace and harmony. If you do not sow, you will not reap. We would look like fools expecting fruits if we till the ground but plant nothing. If you desire a change in your situation, then sow a seed.

The second principle of seedtime and harvest is this: You will reap the harvest you desire if you stay at it. That is, if you persevere. If you plant the seeds and leave them to grow by themselves without preserving and maintaining them, weeds and animals would take over and you would be left with little or nothing to reap. But if you are diligent at keeping weeds and animals out, while watering the plants and fertilizing the soil, you have consciously and deliberately worked towards a good harvest.

To harvest, you have to stay at it. Keep working at it. In this fast-paced world where everything comes with the "now" syndrome, it seems many don't have the time to sow until when it is convenient. But whether it is convenient or not, you need to sow if you desire a harvest.

The third principle is this: You will reap in a different season and not the same season you sowed. Plant in the spring, harvest in the summer. There is a period between planting and harvesting. For example, after you have sown, it takes time for what you planted to grow into something you can eat or sell.

This same principle is true with spiritual planting; what you are reaping today was planted some time ago. What you are planting today, you will reap sometime in the future.

If you want a financial harvest in your life, you must plant financial seeds. You are not qualified to reap if you did not sow. These days, the devil has deceived many Christians into believing they can't afford to sow financially. He'll do everything possible to keep a believer in fear of giving away their resources. Why? Because he knows how much they stand to gain in both the natural and the spiritual realms. Jesus said, *"Give and you will receive. Your gift will return to you in full measure- pressed down, shaken together to make room for more, running over, and poured into your lap. The amount you give will determine the amount you get back" (Luke 6:38) NLT.*

Wow! This is a liberating revelation! It is the reason the enemy doesn't want you to engage in the art and act of sowing. The devil would do anything possible to erase it from your mind. But that would only be to your detriment because it is promised that while the earth remains, seedtime and harvest will not cease.

What is a seed? Seed is *anything* you give. It can be time, money, resources, faith, hope or love. The most important part of sowing is the heart posture behind the gift. So, when you sow, be sure you are acting as a *good* sower.

Remember this: *"He who sows sparingly and grudgingly will also reap sparingly and grudgingly, and he who sows generously [that blessings may come to someone] will also reap generously and with blessings" (2 Corinthians 9:6) AMP.*

When you give in to sorrow, there is no faith, so there is no return. Therefore, sow your seed in joy and you will reap a harvest!

You need to get aggressive about sowing and reaping your harvest.

"And from the days of John the Baptist until the present time, the kingdom of heaven has endured violent assault, and violent men seize it by force [as a precious prize—a share in the heavenly kingdom is sought with most ardent zeal and intense exertion]" (Matthew 11:12) AMP.

Now, there is a major misconception about the principles of sowing and reaping. It is that, after we have sown the seed, we will still need to wait for God to do the reaping for us. When we do this, we miss a very important part we are to play!

We sow the seed, and God gives the increase, but *we* are to reap (or gather) the harvest! In other words, you must become both a sower and a reaper. To reap your harvest, you must become an aggressive reaper. If you leave your harvest in the fields, it will rot!

Make a firm decision today to become aggressive about harvesting. Do not leave anything for the enemy to steal, it belongs to you! For every seed you've ever sown, the harvest is available.

Chapter Four

DESTINY CHANGER

It's your time and turn for a miracle. God is a destiny changer. He holds time and seasons in the palm of His hands. He has the power to transform, alter and change any situation. You must not believe the negative report of the enemies over God's Word. Maintain your faith and have positive expectations that all things will work together for your good. Don't be weary in your faith walk.

Nothing can stop your testimony from manifesting when it's your time and turn for a miracle. Protocols will be broken, burdens lifted, every curse abrogated and God takes all the glory.

MIRACLE AT THE POOL

John 5:1-9: "*After this there was a feast of the Jews; and Jesus went up to Jerusalem. Now there is at Jerusalem by the sheep market a pool, which is called in the Hebrew tongue Bethesda, having five porches. In these lay a great multitude of impotent folk, of blind, halt, withered, waiting for the moving of the water. For an angel went down at a certain season into the pool, and troubled the water: whosoever then first after the troubling of the water stepped in was made whole of whatsoever disease he had. And a certain man was there, which had an infirmity thirty and eight years. When Jesus saw him lie, and knew that he had been now a long time in that case, he saith unto him, Wilt thou be made whole? The impotent man answered him, Sir, I have no man, when the water is troubled, to put me into the pool: but while I am coming, another steppeth down before me. Jesus saith unto him, Rise, take up thy bed, and walk. And immediately the man was made whole, and took up his bed, and walked: and on the same day was the sabbath.*"

The man at the pool is a perfect example of how God can alter a man's season and destiny. 38 years is a long time to sit on a mat. Every day was the same- waiting, watching and hoping. Not much changed. Sitting on the mat had become a way of life for this man. His life was stagnant.

He could not see that the deep well of life was within him. He was convinced that life would bubble up only outside of him and over there, in the magic pool of water. So, he sits on his mat waiting, watching, and hoping that things would change. Then, Jesus asked him, *"Wilt thou be made whole?"* When God asks questions, it is not because he does not know the answers. He asks questions to get us headed back in the right direction.

The man was waiting for the stirring of the water, with just one intention in mind- to get in first because he wanted healing. Sometimes, however, the long process of waiting can deaden our fervency and desire. We can end up more engrossed in the waiting than in the expectation as not everyone waiting has expectations.

Therefore, we need to refer back to the original purpose of being where we are. We need to rediscover our intense desire and longing for what brought us to where we are presently. Tradition has a way of desensitizing our desire, lessening our longings, inhibiting our insight and reducing us to religion that no longer recognizes reality when it stands by us asking the question, *"Wilt thou be made whole?"*

We have waited a long time beside our traditional pool, jealously watching it, pitifully hoping in it, vainly waiting on it, and yet nothing has happened. Our traditions and built-up knowledge have produced nothing but a routine resignation to our ritualistic waiting and hoping.

Sometimes, our long wait becomes a habit and we begin to accept that lifestyle as the norm. So, the enemy imperceptibly tightens the knot on our challenges that we are not even aware that we have increased our burden and pain.

Therefore, we live life gradually adjusting to the pain, sorrow, hurt, and disappointments and wrap them up in layers of resignation, and fatalism, accepting them as the normality of our existence. We end up living with bundles of hurts and disappointments that weigh us down heavily and severely. Thus, limiting our effectiveness. Yet we treat them as an accepted part of our everyday existence. They have become like our old friends whom we will miss if they are not there.

Bethesda means house of mercy or kindness but we need more than kindness to bring deliverance! The pool, though always there, was only stirred at certain times and seasons. However, the times of stirring were the only times it became effective for healing.

The pool has been likened to the logos of God's Word from which we occasionally obtain a Rhema that produces healing. So, we wait and wait for another stirring which may or may not happen in our lifetime.

Like the man at the pool, can we afford the wait?

When the man encountered Jesus, he did not have to wait for a stirring in the pool anymore. This is because Jesus is the embodiment of healing, miracles, deliverance and faith! *"And the Word was made flesh, and dwelt among us, (and we beheld his glory, the glory as of the only begotten of the Father,) full of grace and truth"* (John 1:14).

"He was in the world, and the world was made by him, and the world knew him not. He came unto his own, and his own received him not. But as many as received him, to them gave he power to become the sons of God, even to them that believe on his name: Which were born, not of blood, nor of the will of the flesh, nor of the will of man, but of God" (John 1:10-13).

At the pool, the man had possession of something that activated his healing. The man was patient as he waited for the time he could take advantage of the stirring. He was awaiting his season. He did not complain and had probably accepted the inevitable- that he would be there for a long time. But he was committed to waiting. He was not complaining. He seemed to have cheerfully accepted that he may never get to his goal but he waited anyhow.

For 38 years, he laid there with no one to assist him into the pool but he never gave up. We are used to seeing hopelessness and discouragement in this man but if you study this chapter critically, you will see something else; a hope and a faith that would not give up. It is possible that perhaps, one day, he would have made it to the water thereby getting healed. Maybe one day your traditional expectations may bring fruit but are you really content with waiting that long? The man lived in hope, hoping that one day, it would be his turn.

And one day, his miracle appeared in person and asked *"Wilt thou be made whole?"* Do you really want it? How bad do you really want it? The man had to do something- he had to obey! Who knew a miracle could occur?

The man did not know who Jesus was, so Jesus had to take the initiative to meet the man because he knew all the man needed was a miracle. Not knowing who Jesus was, the man still obeyed because an encounter with Jesus always does something special. His destiny was altered radically.

Do you know who Jesus is? Do you have a long-standing relationship with Him? Have your circumstances degenerated into a hopeless wait because your healing seems to tarry? Have you slid into a gradual acceptance of your state while the enemy gleefully takes advantage of your resignation to wait without expectations?

Luke 18:7-8 says, *"And shall not God avenge his own elect, which cry day and night unto him, though he bear long with them? I tell you that he will avenge them speedily. Nevertheless, when the Son of man cometh, shall he find faith on the earth?"*

Many Christians are still sitting on the sidelines waiting in queue for the stirring of the pool, hoping to get into it for their healing. And they've been sitting or lying there for a long time with nothing happening. They have continued to tarry by their respective pools waiting in vain for a stirring. They are afraid to move for fear that they will miss their chance. God is the God of times and seasons. All you need is God, and God is all you need.

Do you know that God still changes impossible and hopeless situations? Do you know that He still moves the unmovable and shakes the unshakeable? He does not need to consult your past to bless and alter your destiny. He can make your future glorious despite your ugly past. In the place of disappointment, God can give you a destiny appointment. He can prolong your days on the face of the earth.

2 Kings 20:1-6: *In those days was Hezekiah sick unto death. And the prophet Isaiah the son of Amoz came to him, and said unto him, Thus saith the LORD, Set thine house in order; for thou shalt die, and not live. Then he turned his face to the wall, and prayed unto the LORD, saying, I beseech thee, O LORD, remember now how I have walked before thee in truth and with a perfect heart, and have done that which is good in thy sight. And Hezekiah wept sore. And it came to pass, afore Isaiah was gone out into the middle court, that the word of the LORD came to him, saying, Turn again, and tell Hezekiah the captain of my people, Thus saith the LORD, the God of David thy father, I have heard thy prayer, I have seen thy tears: behold, I will heal thee: on the third day thou shalt go up unto the house of the LORD. And I will add unto thy days fifteen years, and I will deliver thee and this city out of the hand of the king of Assyria, and I will defend this city for my own sake, and my servant David's sake."*

Hezekiah was a good man. He was one of the greatest kings that Judah ever had. He had achieved great things. He was always ready to turn to God for help. God had blessed him in an unimaginable way. He was exceedingly wealthy and blessed with much wealth and riches. He was living his life the best he knew how.

But one day, things changed. *"In those days was Hezekiah sick unto death. And the prophet Isaiah the son of Amoz came to him, and said unto him, Thus saith the LORD, Set thine house in order; for thou shalt die, and not live"* (2 Kings 20:1).

In 'those days' when everything was going so well, things changed. And it did not come at a good time, because Judah was being invaded. At the very moment he needed to be strong for the nation, things changed in his personal situation and a deadly illness struck.

It is natural for things to change in our lives. Life is unpredictable, but God is a good God.

Life is unpredictable, but God can be depended on. Life is unpredictable, but our Lord is a destiny changer. Life is unpredictable, but God is always faithful!

In the midst of all of this, the prophet arrived and gave him the worst possible news and the best possible advice. The first was truly dreadful news. In those days, the words of the prophet were direct words from God Himself. The prophet spoke with authority and said "Thus *says the Lord!*" He then gave him this terrible news, *"for you shall die and not recover."*

At the same time, he gave him the best advice under the circumstances, *"Set your house in order".* Was there something not in order? We didn't get much information, but that instruction was given.

The best thing we can do is to ensure that we "keep our house in order". It is vital to keep your house in order. Don't say, "I will get things in order at some later stage". You may not get the opportunity that Hezekiah got.

Live a righteous life. Do the right thing. Stay on the straight and narrow course, and live a life that honors God every day.

A SUPERNATURAL REVERSAL

In that difficult situation, Hezekiah turned to God. When we face difficult situations, the best thing we can do is to turn to God. 2 Kings 20:2 *says "Then Hezekiah turned his face to the wall and prayed to the Lord."* Hezekiah obviously had a personal relationship with God. Hezekiah realized that he needed divine intervention, he needed a miracle.

When we need a miracle in our lives or situations, we should turn to the Lord. It's interesting to note that Hezekiah turned his face to the wall.

He looked away from anything and everything else that may have been a source of hope.

This was the prayer he prayed *"Please, O Lord, remember now [with compassion] how I have walked before You in faithfulness and truth and with a whole heart [entirely devoted to You], and have done what is good in Your sight"* (2Kings 20:3a).

It's a very interesting prayer. At face value, it could appear to be self-righteous but it was far from that. He said "Lord, I've tried to do the right thing and live in a way that pleases You. Please remember me now with compassion." He prayed for himself. Often, we think others must pray for us. As good as this may be, we can also pray for ourselves and over our personal situations, knowing that God hears those prayers too. 2 Kings 20:3b *says "And Hezekiah wept bitterly"*. Sometimes it's not the length of the prayer that matters, but rather the weight of the prayer.

Hezekiah was faced with an impossible situation. He realized the magnitude of the situation that he and the nation faced. The nation was being attacked, the king was deadly sick and there was no heir. This is the worst possible position for a king to be in. But he prayed and wept to God. In the midst of all of this, God intervened.

2 Kings 20:4-5 says *"Before Isaiah had gone out of the middle courtyard, the word of the Lord came to him, saying, "Go back and tell Hezekiah the leader of My people, 'Thus says the Lord, the God of David your father (ancestor): "I have heard your prayer; I have seen your tears. Behold, I am healing you; on the third day you shall go up to the house of the Lord."*

The prophet was on his way out of the palace and halfway across the courtyard when the Lord changed everything and sent him back with the best news ever. There was a supernatural reversal. Never underestimate your calling and prayers to God. The prophet must have been confused. It is almost as if the prayers of Hezekiah changed the mind of God. Hezekiah was a descendant of David. This was a very important fact!

Then God promised to turn both his health and the nation's situation around. 2 Kings 20:6 says *"I will add fifteen years to your life and save you and this city [Jerusalem] from the hand of the king of Assyria; and I will protect this city for My own sake and for my servant David's sake."* Here, we notice the Lord said *"for my servant David's sake."*

Years before, God had made promises to David, so He was not only healing a man and saving a nation, but He was also being faithful to the promises He had made to those who had gone before him.

Perhaps things have happened in the past and you wish you could turn back the hands of the clock or get a second chance. Do not worry, God can turn back the clock in your situation.

He can turn back the clock on the shadow of lost opportunities.

He can turn back the clock on the shadow of mistakes we have made.

He can turn back the clock on the shadow of wasted time.

He can turn back the clock on the shadow of happier days.

He can turn back the clock on the shadow of lost loved ones for we shall see them again (one day) if they too have followed God.

"So I will restore to you the years that the swarming locust has eaten, the crawling locust, and the consuming locust, and the chewing locust, my great army which I sent among you" (Joel 2:25) NKJV.

No matter how bad or ugly your situation might seem, I prophetically announce to you that God is turning around the times and the seasons of your life in your favour in Jesus' name. Every pronouncement of poverty and death against you is terminated from your life in Jesus' name.

PROPHETIC ANNOUNCEMENT

- In the name of Jesus:
- You will not die broke.
- You will not die in poverty.
- You will not die childless.
- You will not die jobless.
- You will not be weak.
- You will not be without direction.
- You will not fail.
- You will rise.
- You will shine.
- You will live.
- You will multiply.
- You will eat the good of the land.
- You will possess the land.
- You will outlive your enemies.
- You will fulfill your purpose.
- You will overcome.
- You will triumph.
- You will dance again.
- You will smile again.

- You will sing again.
- You will win again.
- You will shout for joy again.

God is turning the season around for your lifting.

Because He is: *"Jesus Christ the same yesterday, and today, and for ever" (Hebrews 13:8).*

MAXIMISING YOUR TIME AND SEASONS OF LIFE

God created times and seasons to guide our actions and activities.

"And let us not be weary in well doing: for in due season we shall reap, if we faint not" (Galatians 6:9).

Proverbs 6:6-11

6. Go to the ant, thou sluggard; consider her ways, and be wise:

7. Which having no guide, overseer, or ruler,

8. Provideth her meat in the summer, and gathereth her food in the harvest.

9. How long wilt thou sleep, O sluggard? when wilt thou arise out of thy sleep?

10. Yet a little sleep, a little slumber, a little folding of the hands to sleep:

11. So shall thy poverty come as one that travelleth, and thy want as an armed man.

Your success or failure in life depends on your right use of times and seasons. What the ants do by design, we must do by intention. We must plant in the right season to qualify for the harvest.

Psalms 1:1-3: *"Blessed is the man that walketh not in the counsel of the ungodly, nor standeth in the way of sinners, nor sitteth in the seat of the scornful. But his delight is in the law of the LORD; and in his law doth he meditate day and night. And he shall be like a tree planted by the rivers of water, that bringeth forth his fruit in his season; his leaf also shall not wither; and whatsoever he doeth shall prosper."*

When you make the proper use of your time, you will not miss your season. You will be productive in your season and whatsoever you do will prosper. There is a difference between human timing and God's timing. Physical timing and spiritual timing are different too. Usually, we know a lot about physical timing but God doesn't always tell us about the timing of spiritual visitations or events. Therefore, we greatly need to be spiritually sensitive and physically prepared because when preparation meets opportunity, success is inevitable.

"He hath made everything beautiful in his time: also he hath set the world in their heart, so that no man can find out the work that God maketh from the beginning to the end" (Ecclesiastes 3:11).

There is a time for separation, isolation, preparation, planting and building. Usually, these times are not visible to the public. They are not palatable times. But there is also a time for beautification and glorification. These are times when God puts the spotlight on you to showcase His wonders and glory in your life.

God's time is the best and this is why we must trust God's judgment and timing. This is why you must be deliberate in waiting on God no matter the pressures of life.

"Wait on the LORD: be of good courage, and he shall strengthen thine heart: wait, I say, on the LORD" (Psalm 27:1).

Strength comes when we courageously wait for God's timing in our lives. Also, perspective is maintained.

FAITH IN GOD'S INTEGRITY

We must intentionally train our spirit and mind to trust in God's integrity to bring us into our seasons of fulfillment and glorious joy.

"Who is like unto thee, O LORD, among the gods? who is like thee, glorious in holiness, fearful in praises, doing wonders?" (Exodus 15:11).

He is the God of Israel and the Father of our Lord Jesus Christ. There is no other God besides Him. He is the God who made Heaven and Earth. He is the King of kings and the Lord of lords. He is all-present, all-powerful, all-knowing and all-sufficient.

He knows and reveals hidden and secret things. He is the Creator of times and seasons. He sets and controls times and seasons. Set time is God's time or the divinely set time God sends down his power, grace and glory. God has set times.

THE GOD WHO ALTERS SEASONS

Oftentimes, before God moves us into a new season, He strips us of our past. Putting the past behind us is one of the vital factors required to enter into a new season. In life, sometimes, you must subtract before adding and add before subtracting. You must let go of the past no matter how good, bad or ugly it might seem. Before two individuals decide to get married, they must first decide to let go of some of the ways singles do things if their marriage must thrive.

You cannot get to your destination looking backward. You will crash your present possibilities and hinder your future realities if you focus on the rear view of life. Each time we drive a car, our attention must be on where we are now, and where we are heading. If our focus is on where we have been, it will cause us to crash and may lead to terrible injuries or death. You have to mentally and prayerfully let go of some things to grasp what God has for you in the days ahead. Let go of hurts, let go of failures, let go of letdowns.

As we journey in life, we can glance back but we should always focus forward. Too many have become prisoners of their past. They have allowed themselves to let what happened in the past hinder their future. Some Christians carry their past around like a sack full of stones, thus, slowing them down. If you keep throwing stones at every dog that is barking at you, you will never get to your desired destination. Those who live in ruts dwell on their pasts. Don't dwell on your past. It is gone forever!

If you are in a harsh season, there is hope. The season can change in your favour. The prophet Daniel declared by the inspiration of the Holy Spirit *"He changeth the times and the seasons"* (Daniel 2:21).

"Remember ye not the former things, neither consider the things of old. Behold, I will do a new thing; now it shall spring forth; shall ye not know it? I will even make a way in the wilderness, and rivers in the desert" (Isaiah 43:18-19).

"Brethren, I count not myself to have apprehended: but this one thing I do, forgetting those things which are behind, and reaching forth unto those things which are before" (Philippians 3:13).

DON'T BE CAUGHT IN THE COMPARISON TRAP

Comparing your season to someone else's can lead to great frustration and disappointment. Comparing your life with that of another person can kill contentment and drain the energy in your life. Your season will surely come.

If you buy your dream car today, or next week, you will see someone else with a feature of the car you will wish you had. It is the same way with seasons of life. You will always see someone in a different season than the one you are in, and it will make you envious if you are not careful.

I don't know what season you are in, but most likely, there are people you know whose season you covet. Most of us wish we could be very famous, popular and great. What these unhealthy passions do is make you discontent with your season. Be satisfied with your season. Comparison kills contentment. It is a dangerous thing because you cannot pray away a season.

"He hath made every thing beautiful in his time: also he hath set the world in their heart, so that no man can find out the work that God maketh from the beginning to the end" (Ecclesiastes 3:11).

Here are other versions:

NIV:

"He has made everything beautiful in its time. He has also set eternity in the hearts of men; yet they cannot fathom what God has done from beginning to end."

MSG:

"True, God made everything beautiful in itself and in its time—but he's left us in the dark, so we can never know what God is up to, whether he's coming or going."

THE UNCHANGEABLES

There are unchangeable factors in God's operation. Your role is to come into alignment with divine order. You can't pray away some seasons of life. For example, you can't pray away being a child, a teenager, a senior citizen, or the reality that goes along with those seasons of life. God makes all things beautiful in His time. Each season has its unique reason and beauty. Discontentment may get you to try and force yourself out of a season that you need.

To get into your God-ordained season, two vital factors must be in place:

1.   You must humbly submit to the sovereignty of God.

    "Humble yourselves therefore under the mighty hand of God, that he may exalt you in due time" (1 Peter 5:6).

2.   You must fight the good fight of faith.

    "Fight the good fight of faith, lay hold on eternal life, whereunto thou art also called, and hast professed a good profession before many witnesses" (1 Timothy 6:12).

There are some seasons God would neither make easier nor explain why, as you might not be able to grasp it. The future is clear to God, and uncertain to us. So, it is best to trust the One who knows. Even when we do not understand what God is doing, we must still hold His Hand and trust Him. We must stay in faith trusting in the wisdom of God.

Faithfulness is staying true no matter the season you are in. If God has ordained a season, you cannot change it, but you can decide to get everything you can out of it. Cooperate with the Holy Spirit in this season and take courage because better times are coming!

CHAPTER FIVE

A SHIFT IN THE ATMOSPHERE

This chapter is a prophetic chapter to stir your spirit up because God is about to bring you into a shift. When there is a shift in the atmosphere, your drought will cease and you can be certain that the season is about to change. There was a drought in the land of Israel and God told the prophet that the season was about to change and that rain would be abundant.

In the journey of life, there comes a time in every believer's life when they will experience dryness or drought. A time of loneliness. A time of lack. A time when all we have is a wing and a prayer.

Are you experiencing a drought in your finances?

Are you experiencing drought in your relationships?

Are you experiencing drought in your profession?

Perhaps, you are dying of thirst right now. You are spiritually dehydrated or experiencing deprivation right now. Your change is coming! The atmosphere is about to break.

I want to prophetically announce to you that the *"Drought is over, and the rain is going to fall and permeate every aspect of your life."* There's a time and a season for everything. So, if the drought had a time and season, then know that God's abundance has its time and season as well! Fine, all you see may be a dry, fallow and desert ground. But guess what? It is not what I see concerning you! Instead, I see a dark and heavy cloud, I hear the sound of *"ABUNDANCE OF RAIN."*

Faith cometh by hearing and hearing by the Word of God. We walk by faith or the conception of what we heard and not by what we see. You might see a desert situation, but I dare you to hear the sound of abundance! Abundance comes from the Greek word *"huper-bole"* meaning **"throwing beyond; exceeding greatness; still more excellent; more and more exceeding excellence."**

I prophesy into your life that you will experience a shift from dryness into more than enough, from unproductivity to more and more exceeding excellence. With the unction of the Holy Spirit, I speak exceeding greatness into your family, joy and understanding into your relationships. I speak exceeding excellence into your career and finances.

YOUR DAY WILL BREAK!

If you can hold on just a little longer, the rain will come. Your day will break! The Bible says *"God's anger endures but a moment; in his favor is life; Weeping may* (not "will" but may; a probability not a matter of certainty) *but joy cometh in the morning!"* That's the part we miss.

When the clock hits midnight, tomorrow morning has just begun and a new day has started. Though it is still dark, it is morning already. The stars are still shining but it is morning. The moon is out but it is still morning. The sun has come up but it is still morning. Everybody is still sleeping but it is morning.

However, to activate the shift in your atmosphere, to release the abundance, you must learn to persevere in the place of prayer. Praying in the spirit is the perfect kind of prayer that will rend the heavens open.

While in the place of persistent and prevailing prayer, Elijah sent his servant seven times to look at the atmosphere. Perseverance is one of the keys to making progress in life. It qualifies you for your season of reward. It comes from the Greek word *"proskarteresis"*, meaning "to continue doing something despite opposition."

Don't be comfortable in a season of dryness, set your mind on abundance. Move in the power and strength of the Spirit. Every trying time is a season that will precede the victory. This is why you should *"Count it all joy when you fall into divers temptations;*

knowing that the trying of your faith worketh endurance. But let endurance have her perfect work, that you may be perfected and complete wanting nothing" (James 1:2-4).

Get ready to shout.

Get ready to get your praise on.

Get ready to lift holy hands.

Get ready to dance straight through your drought into abundance.

Can you imagine the task and stress Elijah's servant went through? Six times, the servant heeded the same instruction. Six times, he went by the same process and did the same thing. Six times, the servant came back with the same answer. But the seventh time, he had the same instruction, the same process, but a different outcome.

The seventh time, he saw the shift in the atmosphere.

Oftentimes it's the motivation to keep that produces the miracles we desire. Paul said, "I'm pressing, I'm straining to get to the abundance." You have to press to enter into your season of celebration, reward and victory. You can't afford not to press. This is because, sometimes, the season won't change until you press.

A woman had an issue of blood for 12 years, when she pressed her way to Jesus, she made contact with her miracle. One vital factor you need to know is that before abundance is poured out, you have to perceive it or see it with the eyes of faith. In the case of Elijah, the servant saw a shift in the atmosphere.

What you perceive is what you possess. Perception is everything. When they perceived that Jesus was the Son of God, they received Him. Your life cannot receive what your mind can't perceive. You cannot receive in your hand what you cannot perceive in your mind. There can't be a total possession until there is total perception.

You have to get it in your mind to get it in your hand. To **"Perceive"** comes from the Greek word *"epiginosko."* It means **"to gain a full knowledge of or by experience or observation."**

With all the happenings around the world and in your life, what can you see? I dare you to see the right things.

I dare you to see your deliverance.

I dare you to see your breakthrough. I dare you to see your miracle.

I dare you to see yourself coming out of doubt. I dare you to see yourself paying off your house.

I dare you to see yourself driving that dream car. I dare you to see your children living right.

If you can see it, you can have it. You can't afford not to see it. You can't afford to see your household unsaved. You can't. Begin to see it now.

"And the LORD said unto Abram, after that Lot was separated from him, Lift up now thine eyes, and look from the place where thou art northward, and southward, and eastward, and westward: For all the land which thou seest, to thee will I give it, and to thy seed forever" *(Genesis 13:14-15).*

As the seed of Abraham and heir of the promise, you have the covenant right to see into the realm of the Spirit with the eyes of the Spirit and secure your destiny. In the same way, God promised Abraham in the days of old, He has also promised you that **"whatever you can see, you can have."** What you see is what you get, and you haven't even seen all God has in store for you yet.

"But as it is written, Eye hath not seen, nor ear heard, neither have entered into the heart of man, the things which God hath prepared for them that love him. But God hath revealed them unto us by his Spirit: for the Spirit searcheth all things, yea, the deep things of God" *(1 Corinthians 2:9-10).*

With the eyes of faith, you have to see yourself walking into a new season. With the eyes of faith, you have to see yourself walking into a new day.

With the eyes of faith, you have to see yourself walking into a new dimension.

With the eyes of faith, you have to see yourself in the congregation of the great, high and mighty.

With the eyes of faith, you have to see yourself walking with royalty.

You must have a big vision. When you have a big vision, God is well pleased. This is because a big vision will attract His mighty power. Make sure you write your vision down and make it plain; for the vision is yet for an appointed time, but at the end, it shall speak and not lie: it will surely come.

Your vision will come to pass. And because it will come to pass, you have to be prepared for it so that you will not miss your season when it comes.

The word "prepare" comes from the Greek word "proetsimazo" meaning "to be completely furnished." You have to be furnished with the Word. You must be furnished with the anointing.

No matter the global economic meltdown and pandemic, I prophesy over you that the drought is over in your life!

Live life to the fullest now because the drought is over! Praise God now because the drought is over!

Shout for joy and victory because the drought is over! Allow yourself to love again because the drought is over! Sing again because the drought is over!

Pray now because the drought is over! Preach now because the drought is over! Prophesy now because the drought is over! Plant now because the drought is over Produce now because the drought is over!

A BLESSED ASSURANCE

"My times are in thy hand: deliver me from the hand of mine enemies, and from them that persecute me. Make thy face to shine upon thy servant: save me for thy mercies' sake" (Psalm 31: 15-16).

God is the architect of the universe. He is the First and the Last, the Beginning and the End! He is the unmovable, unchangeable and undefeated Champion. He is the keeper of creation and the Creator of all things. He is in charge of time and seasons of life with His sovereignty and all-powerfulness. The entire Old

Testament was a preparation for the coming of Jesus Christ as prophecy after prophecy told of His coming,

"For unto us a child is born, to us a son is given…and His name will be called Wonderful, Counselor, Mighty God, Everlasting Father, Prince of Peace "(Isaiah 9:6) NKJV.

Then, when this greatly prophesied child came to the world and began His ministry, His initial message began with the words: *"The time is fulfilled, and the Kingdom of God is at hand; repent and believe in the Gospel."* It was Jesus' way of saying my Heavenly Father is in charge of time.

"It is not for you to know times or seasons which the Father has fixed by His own authority" (Acts 1:7) (AMP). This was the same message Jesus had given much earlier to His followers when He talked about His second coming:

"But of that day and hour no one knows, not even the angels of heaven, nor the Son but the Father only" (Matthew 24:36) NKJV.

And this sovereignty and control that God has over time, season and history, does not apply to just a general understanding of life but applies quite specifically to each believer's personal lives.

"Seeing his days are determined, the number of his months are with thee, thou hast appointed his bounds that he cannot pass" (Job 14:5).

Psalms 139:16-18: *Thine eyes did see my substance, yet being unperfect; and in thy book all my members were written, which in continuance were fashioned, when as yet there was none of them. How precious also are thy thoughts unto me, O God! how great is the sum of them If I should count them, they are more in number than the sand: when I awake, I am still with thee."*

Before we were born, God had already decided the number of days we would spend on Earth. God is in charge not just of time, but of my time and yours as well. My times are in His hand. If you and I can believe that and trust God to be a loving God, you won't need to fear or worry.

This is because, there is comfort and assurance in knowing that God is not only in control but is in control of each day, each hour that we have to live on Earth and for all eternity.

God is concerned about the details of every minute of our everyday life. Oftentimes, we think God is too busy with much more important matters than to be concerned about "minor" and "small" incidents. This is a false belief. God cares about every detail of our lives. There was a time Jesus needed some tax money. He told Peter to go to the sea and cast a hook and for the first fish that was caught, he was to open its mouth and take out a shekel. And it was so (Matthew 17:27).

Matthew 10:29-31

29. Are not two sparrows sold for a farthing? and one of them shall not fall on the ground without your Father.

30. But the very hairs of your head are all numbered.

31. Fear ye not therefore, ye are of more value than many sparrows.

Jesus said even the hairs on your head are all numbered. The timing of God reaches from before the beginning of time to all of eternity measuring out the lives of nations and empires. It also made ready the coming and the second coming of His Son. But included in the timing of this great salvation history is His attention given to the smallest details-the length of life of a hair on your head. Your times are in the hand of God.

GOD IS UNCHANGEABLE

No matter how ugly or bad your situation might seem, God is in control. Sometimes you might not understand what God is doing in your life. Perhaps, it seemed like God was blessing you, but after a while, it felt like He wasn't anymore. Or it seemed like your prayers were being answered, but now it seems like they aren't. For you, things used to be easy, but now it seems like they are hard and impossible. You might be wondering, "why are these happening and what is God doing about them?"

Let me announce to you that you are in a season.

Every man on the face of the Earth is in different seasons of life.

Some are new parents; others have become empty nesters.

Some have just started a new job; others are getting ready to retire.

While some are dating, another is newly married, divorced, or are hitting 30 years of marriage.

Some are new believers in Christ, while some aren't sure if they're Christians. Some are back in church after a long time away, while some are church leaders. We're all in different seasons of life.

Therefore, the book of Solomon talks about seasons because the way we experience life is in seasons.

PREDESTINATED

You are a product of divine intention and conclusion. God had decided your destiny, times and seasons of life before you were ever born. You have been predestinated by God.

Now, God brings different seasons into our lives at different times. For some, we wish we could stay in forever, and for others, we wish we could skip completely. But one of the most comforting things about God is that He makes everything beautiful in his time. Ecclesiastes 3:11-12 says *"He has made everything **BEAUTIFUL IN HIS TIME."*** Notice the words, "in his time." He has also set eternity in the heart of man, yet no one can fathom what God has done from beginning to end.

This was an incredible revelation that God gave to Solomon, but as New Testament saints, we have an advantage over Solomon because we have God's Word and the Holy Spirit that he didn't have.

"Having made known unto us the mystery of his will, according to his good pleasure which he hath purposed in himself: That in the dispensation of the fullness of times he might gather together in one all things in Christ, both which are in heaven, and which are on earth; even in him:" (Ephesians 1:9-10).

Paul was describing God's ultimate purpose to bring everything in Heaven and Earth under the rule of Christ. The book of Ecclesiastes speaks about how it's often difficult to figure out God's purpose in the seasons of our lives.

However, Paul came along a little later and said that, now that Christ has been born, died for us and was raised from the dead, we can now know the purpose of God in every season. The ultimate purpose is to bring everything under the rule of Christ, both in Heaven and on Earth.

This means that the seasons of your life are not an accident. There is a divine timing for everything that happens in your life, and if we can understand this, it will remove all worries and anxieties from our lives.

God changes the times and seasons of your life whether you realize it or not. Every season of your life is scheduled by God but he doesn't post the schedule for you to see. And that's what makes living so challenging because we are surrounded by many uncertainties in life. That's why Solomon says "… *yet no one can fathom what God has done from beginning to end.*" No one can see the big picture, except God,

No one can understand all the seasons you pass through, except God. Paul says that from eternity, God has had a purpose that's been working in your life. Your destiny was created in eternity, and God has a plan for it all, but your life is experienced in seasons.

Everything that God wants to do through your life has been decided before your life ever began. But you don't experience everything that God intends for your life, all at once. You experience it in phases and seasons.

Have you ever tried to escape your current season to the next season? We're always itching and waiting to get to the next season because the next season always looks better than our current season. That you are predestinated does not mean you will not face difficult times.

One thing you must realize is that every season has its struggles, those kinds you can't see from the outside while trying to look in. You must break free from the mindset of trying to live in somebody else's season.

TAKING ROOTS DOWNWARD

Before you ascend into dimensions of life, you must first be intentional about taking roots downward. When you are deeply rooted in life, you will be firm and established. If you do a reality check, there is a part of you that looks at other people; the season they're in, the success they enjoy, the height they've reached, and you're thinking, "if I could just get there, then I'd be all right." You need to realize that every season has its unique struggle that you can't see or know until you're in it. And if you get this truth deep down in your spirit, it'll set you free from envy and competitive jealousy.

It'll set you free from always trying to copy someone else's circumstances. The problem is, when we look at other people's lives, we only see how high the tree goes, we don't see how deep the roots are planted. You only see the fruit of what someone has, you don't see the fight they went through to have it. You observe somebody else's season as a visitor, and it looks nice, but it's different when you live there.

Have you ever been to a place you usually love to visit but still wouldn't want to live in? It looks great when you visit, but is quite different when you happen to live there. And that's how it is with the seasons of our lives.

We see people in seemingly nicer and greater seasons than ours, but we don't see the struggles going on. There's a struggle in every season. And the sooner we realize it, the sooner we are set free from unrealistic expectations to enjoy the season that we are in.

SHAPING YOUR SEASONS

The worst of seasons can be the best of seasons if only you know the dynamics of shaping the seasons. Every season is shaped by what you say. You can prolong a miserable season by your disobedience. The departure of the children of Israel from Egypt is a classic example. They turned what should have been a couple-of-weeks journey into a forty-year painful experience.

Sometimes, you can pleasantly alter your season with a simple act of obedience; for example, by deciding to do what God told you to do in the first place.

But there are some seasons where you are waiting on God for a change, but it doesn't happen simply because it's not yet the right time for your next season. In a season like this, you simply have to trust God and endure the pain. Even though you can't control your current season, you can control what you say about it.

God has made everything beautiful in His time. What separates those who walk by faith from those who just wander through life aimlessly? It is what they choose to call the season that they're in.

Do you call your season based on faith and trust in God? Do you believe God can make something beautiful of it? Or do you call your season based on doubt and cynicism? What are you saying about your current season? What are you calling your current season? What you say about your season determines how you will experience that season.

Your season will take on the characteristics of your description of it. So, if you choose to call your season beautiful, it will become beautiful in your eyes. Because you're able to recognize that it is in God's time, and that, God makes everything beautiful in His time.

If you have the right perspective and begin to recognize what God is doing in you, during this season you're in, you will see the beauty in it. You will recognize that, though it is sometimes painful, miserable and discouraging, God is using it for your lifting. If you speak about your season like it is overwhelming, it becomes overwhelming. Also, it becomes devastating if you speak about your season like it is devastating.

This is because the way you speak about your season shapes the way you experience that season. After they departed from Egypt, the people of Israel immediately started complaining and whining. They said *"we want to go back to Egypt"* amongst other unhealthy comments. Therefore, this shaped their next 40 years in the wilderness.

Seasons are critically vital to our success in life. We will all go through them; a season of grace, a season of learning, a season of growing, a season of trial, a season of correction, a season of brokenness, a season of positioning, a season of humbling, a season of elevation and a season of elevating others.

There are times in our lives when God would train and use us and the gifts would pour out of us like warm honey. Also, there are times when we would feel like we're passing through a dry and weary land. All are different seasons of life.

"O God, thou art my God; early will I seek thee: my soul thirsteth for thee, my flesh longeth for thee in a dry and thirsty land, where no water is;" (Psalms 63:1).

No matter how dry your season might seem, you must stay connected to God. Because He makes everything beautiful in His time. So, even if you're in a miserable season, see it as a time of growth and development for your next level.

Having the right perception about your current season will open your eyes to see the growth God is doing in you, thereby shaping the way you experience your season. Even if you're in a season that seems difficult, see it as an opportunity to build into other people and help other people. This mindset will open your eyes to see the people that God has placed around you to be influenced by you.

Now, let's do this exercise. Say after me:

I call my current season beautiful.

I call my current season glorious.

I call my current season blessed.

I call my current season prosperous.

I call my current season great.

I call my current season awesome.

I call my current season excellent.

I call my current season the school of the Spirit.

I call my current season the "I am under construction" phase.

You must realize that God is working in and for you.

The way you talk about your season will align your attitude with the right words.

You cannot control your season but you can control your attitude. You can change your perspective. You can change your mindset. Be determined to speak God's promises over your season. Speak about God's faithfulness in your season, then God will open your eyes to see the beauty in it. Because God makes everything beautiful in His time.

"Blessed is the man that walketh not in the counsel of the ungodly, nor standeth in the way of sinners, nor sitteth in the seat of the scornful. But his delight is in the law of the LORD; and in his law doth he meditate day and night. And he shall be like a tree planted by the rivers of water, that bringeth forth his fruit in his season; his leaf also shall not wither; and whatsoever he doeth shall prosper" (Psalms 1:1-3).

Don't get discouraged, your season of manifestation will surely come. Don't get discontented in your waiting season. Don't wander away from God's will because you think the season you're in is unbearable. Don't wander away from God, stay connected to Him because when it's your time, you don't want to miss your turn. When your turn comes, you want to be ready for it. Don't miss your turn.

Be sensitive because God makes everything beautiful in His time. You can't live in the season that was, and you can't make the next season come right now, but there is a strength in your current season that you can take advantage of. You can't live in someone else's season. You might not have what you used to have; you might not get what you want to get. But if you choose to plant your roots deep down in God's purpose for you, He will make your life glorious.

CHAPTER SIX

THE SET TIME

"Thou shalt arise, and have mercy upon Zion: for the time to favour her, yea, the set time, is come" (Psalm 102:13).

There are set times for every believer in Christ. A set time is the time of God's visitation. God's set time is different from man's time. Our set times are different from one to another. My time is different from yours. It's a case of different strokes for different folks.

Let's see some examples from the scriptures on the set times of God.

ABRAHAM AND SARAH

Genesis 18:10, 14

10. And he said, I will certainly return unto thee according to the time of life; and, lo, Sarah thy wife shall have a son. And Sarah heard it in the tent door, which was behind him.

14. Is any thing too hard for the LORD? At the time appointed I will return unto thee, according to the time of life, and Sarah shall have a son.

God told Abraham that He would certainly return according to the TIME OF LIFE to give them the promised child. God is a Man of HIS WORD. Abraham and Sarah waited till old age to have a child according to the set time of God.

"For Sarah conceived, and bare Abraham a son in his old age, at the set time of which God had spoken to him" (Genesis 21:2).

RACHAEL AND LEAH

Genesis 29:31-35

31. And when the LORD saw that Leah was hated, he opened her womb: but Rachel was barren.

32. And Leah conceived, and bare a son, and she called his name Reuben: for she said, Surely the LORD hath looked upon my affliction; now therefore my husband will love me.

33. And she conceived again, and bare a son; and said, Because the LORD hath heard that I was hated, he hath therefore given me this son also: and she called his name Simeon.

34. And she conceived again, and bare a son; and said, Now this time will my husband be joined unto me, because I have born him three sons: therefore was his name called Levi.

35. And she conceived again, and bare a son: and she said, Now will I praise the LORD: therefore she called his name Judah; and left bearing.

Are you being mocked by men that you will die childless?

Are you being mocked that you are a failure?

Are you being talked about and ostracized? Here is the good news:

God will use the mockery of men to make you.

God will use the mockery of men to give you a testimony.

God will use the mockery of men to make you a star.

God will use the mockery of men to make you a global phenomenon.

God will use the mockery of men to publicize your victory.

God will use the mockery of men as a platform to promote you.

God will use the mockery of men to glorify you.

God will use the mockery of men to beautify you.

To you who has been talked down on and mocked, I say massive congratulations because you are about to enter into victory!

HANNAH

1 Samuel 1:5, 11, 19: *"But unto Hannah he gave a worthy portion; for he loved Hannah: but the LORD had shut up her womb.a vow, and said, O LORD of hosts, if thou wilt indeed look on the affliction of thine handmaid, and remember me, and not forget thine handmaid, but wilt give unto thine handmaid a man child, then I will give him unto the LORD all the days of his life, and there shall no razor come upon his head.*

19. And they rose up in the morning early, and worshipped before the LORD, and returned, and came to their house to Ramah: and Elkanah knew Hannah his wife; and the LORD remembered her.

"And the LORD visited Hannah, so that she conceived, and bare three sons and two daughters. And the child Samuel grew before the LORD." (1 Samuel 2:21).

When it is your set time, God will not only answer your prayers, He will also exceed your expectations. He will give you in abundance more than what you need. God shut Hannah's womb because He wanted to use her womb to birth prophet Samuel - one of the greatest prophets who ever lived.

Also, the Lord Jesus Christ had His set time but the faith of His mother activated the season of miracles. Faith and obedience to divine instruction will activate your season of miracles.

John 2:3-11

And when they wanted wine, the mother of Jesus saith unto him, They have no wineJesus saith unto her, Woman, what have I to do with thee? mine hour is not yet come.His mother saith unto the servants, Whatsoever he saith unto you, do it. And there were set there six waterpots of stone, after the manner of the purifying of the Jews, containing two or three firkins apiece. Jesus saith unto them, Fill the waterpots with water. And they filled them up to the brim. And he saith unto them, Draw out now, and bear unto the governor of the feast. And they bare it. 9. When the ruler of the feast had tasted the water that was made wine, and knew not whence it was: (but the servants which drew the water knew;) the governor of the feast called the bridegroom, And saith unto him, Every man at the beginning doth set forth good wine; and when men have well drunk, then that which is worse: but thou hast kept the good wine until now. This beginning of miracles did Jesus in Cana of Galilee, and manifested forth his glory; and his disciples believed on him."

Isaiah 55:8-11

8. For my thoughts are not your thoughts, neither are your ways my ways, saith the LORD.

9. For as the heavens are higher than the earth, so are my ways higher than your ways, and my thoughts than your thoughts.

10. For as the rain cometh down, and the snow from heaven, and returneth not thither, but watereth the earth, and maketh it bring forth and bud, that it may give seed to the sower, and bread to the eater:

11. So shall my word be that goeth forth out of my mouth: it shall not return unto me void, but it shall accomplish that which I please, and it shall prosper in the thing whereto I sent it.

There is a sent word of healing, prosperity and blessings for you. But it will take faith and obedience to activate the reality of the Word in your life. God's Word has been given to us to alter our seasons and enjoy all the rich benefits of redemption.

There is a period of prayer as well as the moment of answer. Oftentimes, prayer becomes a challenge because we have not developed the ability to wait for that moment of answer from God. Everybody has their time. So, you must be patient to wait for your set time. Today, make a quality decision to follow God's time and go at His pace.

2 Samuel 5: 22-25

22. And the Philistines came up yet again, and spread themselves in the valley of Rephaim.

23. And when David inquired of the LORD, he said, Thou shalt not go up; but fetch a compass behind them, and come upon them over against the mulberry trees.

24. And let it be, when thou hearest the sound of a going in the tops of the mulberry trees, that then thou shalt bestir thyself: for then shall the LORD go out before thee, to smite the host of the Philistines.

25. And David did so, as the LORD had commanded him; and smote the Philistines from Geba until thou come to Gazer.

Obedience to divine instruction will precede seasons of victory. It is a fatal error and a major mistake to go by other people's time. This is the root of failure in life. You must dare to trust God absolutely. You must never be desperate for anything in life. You must stay in your lane and not compare yourself with others or envy others.

DARE TO PREPARE FOR YOUR SET TIME

"Then Pharaoh sent and called Joseph, and they brought him hastily out of the dungeon: and he shaved himself, and changed his raiment, and came in unto Pharaoh" (Genesis 41:14).

Before your set time, you must be prepared for it. When Joseph was sent for, he shaved and changed his garment because he knew that his set time had come.

The set time is a time of divine visitation.

The set time is a time of fulfillment of dreams.

The set time is a time when the king comes or sends for you.

The set time is a time of favour, reward and just recompense.

The set time is a time of manifestation, elevation and promotion.

We don't know what the future holds but we know it's a glorious future because our times are in God's hands. Though we don't have control over our set times, we must always prepare ourselves and be ready. Joseph didn't know when God would visit him to fulfill his childhood God-given dreams. However, he looked forward in anticipation and prepared himself every time, all along for that time.

15 THINGS TO KNOW ABOUT SET TIMES

1. The set time is God's time or a divinely appointed time.
2. God's set time is different from man's time.
3. It is a fixed time set by God. That is, it is God's fixed time.
4. Set time is a time of remembrance.
5. Set time is God's due time.
6. Set time is maturity, harvest & reward time.
7. Set time is a time of divine visitation.
8. Set time is a time of favour.
9. Set time is the time when sins are forgiven.
10. Set time is the time when yokes are broken.
11. Set time is the time when deliverance comes.
12. Set time is the time when healings take place.
13. Set time is the time when a man is uplifted.
14. Set time is the time when God is glorified.
15. Set time is the time when men are blessed and some people are upset.

FACTORS THAT CAN PREPARE YOU FOR THE SET TIME

1. LIVE BY THE WORD OF GOD

You cannot have lasting and durable success if you do not live by God's Word. The Word empowers and fortifies your spirit. They sustain your spirit and renew your mind. You must feed on the Word daily.

"This book of the law shall not depart out of thy mouth; but thou shalt meditate therein day and night, that thou mayest observe to do according to all that is written therein: for then thou shalt make thy way prosperous, and then thou shalt have good success" (Joshua 1:8).

"Thy word have I hid in mine heart, that I might not sin against thee." (Psalm 119:11)

"But he answered and said, it is written, Man shall not live by bread alone, but by every word that proceedeth out of the mouth of God" (Matthew 4:4).

"Let the word of Christ dwell in you richly in all wisdom; teaching and admonishing one another in psalms and hymns and spiritual songs, singing with grace in your hearts to the Lord" (Colossians 3:16).

2. PRACTISE GODLINESS

Sin is a killer and a blessing-blocker. You must avoid a life of sin and practise godliness.

"Righteousness exalteth a nation: but sin is a reproach to any people" (Proverbs 14:34).

3. BUILD CAPACITY

Your capacity is your ability. Your next level of life is a product of an enlarged capacity. You must be determined to learn. Acquire relevant education and training that will advance your purpose, vision and career. You must get the necessary and adequate knowledge and skills.

"If the iron be blunt, and he do not whet the edge, then must he put to more strength: but wisdom is profitable to direct" (Ecclesiastes 10:10).

"Wisdom is the principal thing; therefore get wisdom: and with all thy getting get understanding. Exalt her, and she shall promote thee: she shall bring thee to honour, when thou dost embrace her. She shall give to thine head an ornament of grace: a crown of glory shall she deliver to thee" (Proverbs 4:7-9).

"Study to shew thyself approved unto God, a workman that needeth not to be ashamed, rightly dividing the word of truth." (2 Timothy 2:15)

4. START EARLY

It is very vital to know what you are called to do early in life. Pursue your vision early. Run with your assignment early. Live a life of purpose early.

"O God, thou art my God; early will I seek thee: my soul thirsteth for thee, my flesh longeth for thee in a dry and thirsty land, where no water is;" (Psalms 63:1).

"I love them that love me; and those that seek me early shall find me" (Proverbs 8:17).

"As arrows are in the hand of a mighty man; so are children of the youth" (Psalms 127:4).

"Remember now thy Creator in the days of thy youth, while the evil days come not, nor the years draw nigh, when thou shalt say, I have no pleasure in them;" (Ecclesiastes 12:1).

5. BE HARD-WORKING, DILIGENT AND RESOURCEFUL

You must have set goals; both long-term and short-term goals. This will give you a sense of direction. However, it is not enough to set goals. You must have set structures that will help you to fulfill your goals. Beyond building structures around your goals, you must be determined to work. Be diligent. Remember, it is not mere men that stand before kings but those who put in the work.

"The hand of the diligent shall bear rule: but the slothful shall be under tribute" (Proverbs 12:24).

"Seest thou a man diligent in his business? he shall stand before kings; he shall not stand before mean men" (Proverbs 22:29).

6. BE PRAYERFUL

Maintain a life of prayer. Give yourself to it.

"And he spake a parable unto them to this end, that men ought always to pray, and not to faint;" (Luke 18:1).

"Pray without ceasing" (2 Thessalonians 5:17).

7. BE SENSITIVE TO OPPORTUNITIES

This is important. Open your eyes to opportunities around you. As you work hard, work smart. Do not let divine opportunities pass by you. Seize them!

"Be ye not as the horse, or as the mule, which have no understanding: whose mouth must be held in with bit and bridle, lest they come near unto thee" (Psalms 32:9).

"The labour of the foolish wearieth every one of them, because he knoweth not how to go to the city" (Ecclesiastes 10:15).

8. BE WILLING TO GIVE AND SERVE

Wherever you find yourself, offer your resources to those around you. Though you can bless people in cash, however, giving is not only restricted to that. You can offer your talent, time etc., as well.

"There is that scattereth, and yet increaseth; and there is that withholdeth more than is meet, but it tendeth to poverty. The liberal

soul shall be made fat: and he that watereth shall be watered also himself. He that withholdeth corn, the people shall curse him: but blessing shall be upon the head of him that selleth it" (Proverbs 11:24-26).

"Give, and it shall be given unto you; good measure, pressed down, and shaken together, and running over, shall men give into your bosom. For with the same measure that ye mete withal it shall be measured to you again" (Luke 6:38).

9. BE FAITHFUL

Faithfulness is what will determine your next responsibility. You must decide to handle your present jobs well. Also, you need to realize that your present job, position & disposition in life is a test from God (Matthew 25: 20-30).

10. BUILD YOUR NETWORK

Success in life is a function of relationships. Opportunities are in people. Therefore, it is vital to connect with people. Network and be friendly in every environment you find yourself.

"A man that hath friends must shew himself friendly: and there is a friend that sticketh closer than a brother" (Proverbs 18:24).

11. LIVE IN JOYFUL EXPECTATION

"Serve the LORD with gladness: come before his presence with singing" (Psalms 100:2).

"Every man according as he purposeth in his heart, so let him give; not grudgingly, or of necessity: for God loveth a cheerful giver" (2 Corinthians 9:7).

SEASON OF REMEMBRANCE

Set time is also a season of remembrance. God is set to remember you in this season of great trials and uncertainties.

Genesis 8:1 said, *"And God remembered Noah ..."*

Genesis 30:22 said, *"And God remembered Rachel, and God hearkened to her, and opened her womb."*

Exodus 2:24, 25 said *"…and God remembered his covenant with Abraham, with Isaac, and with Jacob. And God looked upon the children of Israel, and God had respect unto them."*

When it's your set time, even if men forget you, at set times, God would bring you into their remembrance or remind them about you. God never forgets you.

GENESIS 41:9-14

9. Then spake the chief butler unto Pharaoh, saying, I do remember my faults this day:

10. Pharaoh was wroth with his servants, and put me in ward in the captain of the guard's house, both me and the chief baker:

11. And we dreamed a dream in one night, I and he; we dreamed each man according to the interpretation of his dream.

12. And there was there with us a young man, an Hebrew, servant to the captain of the guard; and we told him, and he interpreted to us our dreams; to each man according to his dream he did interpret.

13. And it came to pass, as he interpreted to us, so it was; me he restored unto mine office, and him he hanged.

14. Then Pharaoh sent and called Joseph, and they brought him hastily out of the dungeon: and he shaved himself, and changed his raiment, and came in unto Pharaoh.

When your set time comes, you will stand before kings and not ordinary men. Set time is a time of divine visitation and uncommon favour. Joseph was called from the prison to the palace, and his destiny was altered by the God of times and seasons.

THE SEASON OF HONOUR
Esther 6:1-11

1. On that night could not the king sleep, and he commanded to bring the book of records of the chronicles; and they were read before the king.

2. And it was found written, that Mordecai had told of Bigthana and Teresh, two of the king's chamberlains, the keepers of the door, who sought to lay hand on the king Ahasuerus.

3. And the king said, What honour and dignity hath been done to Mordecai for this? Then said the king's servants that ministered unto him, There is nothing done for him.

4. And the king said, Who is in the court? Now Haman was come into the outward court of the king's house, to speak unto the king to hang Mordecai on the gallows that he had prepared for him.

5. And the king's servants said unto him, Behold, Haman standeth in the court. And the king said, Let him come in.

6. So Haman came in. And the king said unto him, What shall be done unto the man whom the king delighteth to honor? Now Haman thought in his heart, To whom would the king delight to do honour more than to myself?

7. And Haman answered the king, For the man whom the king delighted to honour,

8. Let the royal apparel be brought which the king useth to wear, and the horse that the king rideth upon, and the crown royal which is set upon his head:

9. And let this apparel and horse be delivered to the hand of one of the king's most noble princes, that they may array the man withal whom the king delighteth to honour, and bring him on horseback through the street of the city, and proclaim before him, Thus shall it be done to the man whom the king delighteth to honour.

10. Then the king said to Haman, Make haste, and take the apparel and the horse, as thou hast said, and do even so to Mordecai the Jew, that sitteth at the king's gate: let nothing fail of all that thou has spoken.

11. Then took Haman the apparel and the horse, and arrayed Mordecai, and brought him on horseback through the street of the city, and proclaimed before him, Thus shall it be done unto the man whom the king delighteth to honor.

Set time is a season of honor. Mordecai and the entire Jewish race were programmed to be destroyed by "Haman", the enemy of the Jews. But the God of times and seasons turned everything around for the favour and the honor of Mordecai. He was honored by the king and Haman was destroyed.

SET TIME OF MANIFESTATION

Isaiah 60:1-3

1. Arise, shine; for thy light is come, and the glory of the LORD is risen upon thee.

2. For, behold, the darkness shall cover the earth, and gross darkness the people: but the LORD shall arise upon thee, and his glory shall be seen upon thee.

3. And the Gentiles shall come to thy light, and kings to the brightness of thy rising.

Set time is a time of manifestation. It is a time to shine and illuminate your world with the glory of God. It is the time when everything and everyone around you will feel and be touched by the life of God in you.

Romans 8:18-19 says, *"For I reckon that the sufferings of this present time are not worthy to be compared with the glory which shall be revealed in us. For the earnest expectation of the creature waiteth for the manifestation of the sons of God."*

Set time is the time to manifest sonship in God. Set time is testimony time!

If you read Ecclesiastes 3:1-8, you will realise that God's set time could take many forms. As humans, it may not always look good or be positive but God's set time is always the time when all things work together for the good of those who love Him. It is a time when all things turn out right, exact, appropriate, fitting and beautiful.

The set time for the wicked could be a time of judgment. It is when wickedness comes to an end. Proverbs 11:21 says, *"Though hand join in hand, the wicked shall not be unpunished: but the seed of the righteous shall be delivered."* Do you remember how Pharaoh and all the Egyptian chariots got drowned in the Red Sea? Do you remember the tragic end of Haman? That is judgement.

THIS IS YOUR SET TIME!

This book in your hands is clear-cut prophetic evidence that this is your set time for a complete turnaround in every dimension of your life.

It is your set time for unprecedented favour!
It is your set time for acceptance!
It is your set time for destiny fulfilment!
It is your set time for divine promotion!
It is your set time for celebration!
It is your set time to win!
It is your set time for perfect healing!
It is your set time for restoration!
It is your set time for total victory!
It is your set time to eat the good of the land!
It is your set time to be celebrated!
It is your set time for glory!
It is your set time for abundance!
It is your set time for prosperity!
It is your set time for open doors!
It is your set time for the supernatural!
It is your set time for manifestation!
It is your set time of remembrance!
It is your set time for honour!

PROPHETIC PRAYERS

I encourage you to make these prophetic declarations with faith and see how God will cause times and seasons to respond favorably to you.

So, say these with me:

1. I declare that in my season of waiting I am strong and filled with courage in Jesus' name.

"Wait for and confidently expect the Lord; Be strong and let your heart take courage; Yes, wait for and confidently expect the Lord" (Psalms 27:14) AMP.

2. I declare that in my season of waiting, I am walking in the truth of God's Word. I am taught by Him, for He is the God of my salvation.

"Lead me in Your truth and teach me, For You are the God of my salvation; On You I wait all the day" (Psalms 25:5) NKJV.

3. I declare that in my season of waiting, I have patience as I await Your imminent return.

"Now as for you, dear brothers who are waiting for the Lord's return, be patient, like a farmer who waits until the autumn for his precious harvest to ripen" (James 5:7) TLB.

4. I declare that in my season of waiting, I am preserved by His integrity and uprightness in every dimension in Jesus' name.

"May integrity and uprightness preserve me, for I wait for You" (Psalms 25:21) ESV.

5. I declare that in my season of waiting, I possess new strength to mount up with wings like eagles. To run and not get tired and walk without becoming weary in Jesus' name.

"But they that wait upon the LORD shall renew their strength; they shall mount up with wings as eagles; they shall run, and not be weary; and they shall walk, and not faint." (Isaiah 40:31)

I become deliberate in sowing for this season in Jesus' name.

I declare I have understanding for this season in Jesus' name.

I declare that I will fulfill the purpose for this season in Jesus' name.

I declare I have insight for this season of my life in Jesus' name.

I declare I will build spiritual strength and capacity for this season in Jesus' name.

I declare I have received clarity for this season in Jesus' name.

I declare I have supernatural understanding in Jesus' name.